Penguins Are Waterbirds

Written by Sharon Taberski
and her first-grade class

Contents

Introduction

Penguins can walk, slide, and swim, but they cannot fly. They are waterbirds.

Kinds of Penguins

There are 17 kinds of penguins.
Here are some of them.

Blue Penguin

Galapagos Penguin

Adélie Penguin

Erect-crested Penguin

Humboldt Penguin

Snares Penguin

This is the biggest kind of penguin.
It can grow to be four feet tall.

Emperor Penguin

This is the smallest kind of penguin.
It can grow to be the size of a small duck.

Blue Penguin

Where Penguins Live

All penguins live in the bottom half of the world.
They live close to the water.

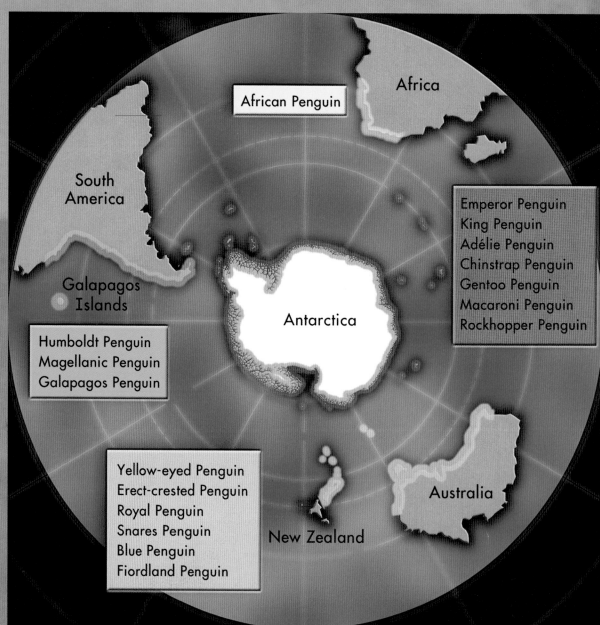

African Penguin

Africa

South
America

Galapagos
Islands

Emperor Penguin
King Penguin
Adélie Penguin
Chinstrap Penguin
Gentoo Penguin
Macaroni Penguin
Rockhopper Penguin

Humboldt Penguin
Magellanic Penguin
Galapagos Penguin

Antarctica

Yellow-eyed Penguin
Erect-crested Penguin
Royal Penguin
Snares Penguin
Blue Penguin
Fiordland Penguin

Australia

New Zealand

map of Earth from South Pole

Some penguins live where it is very cold.
They live on ice and snow.

Some penguins live where it is warmer.
They live on land.

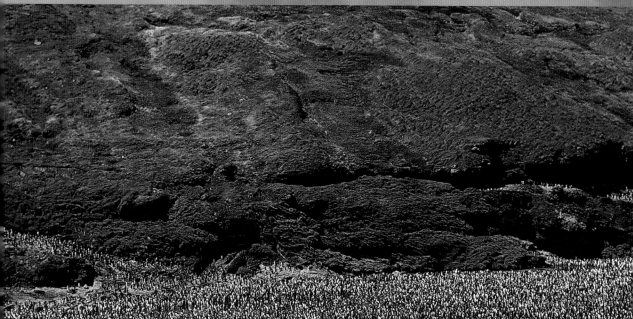

Penguins live on beaches, on islands, and on rocks.

beach

islands

rocks

Parts of a Penguin's Body

Penguins have flippers.

They use their flippers to swim.

flippers

Penguins have webbed feet.
Their webbed feet help them swim fast.

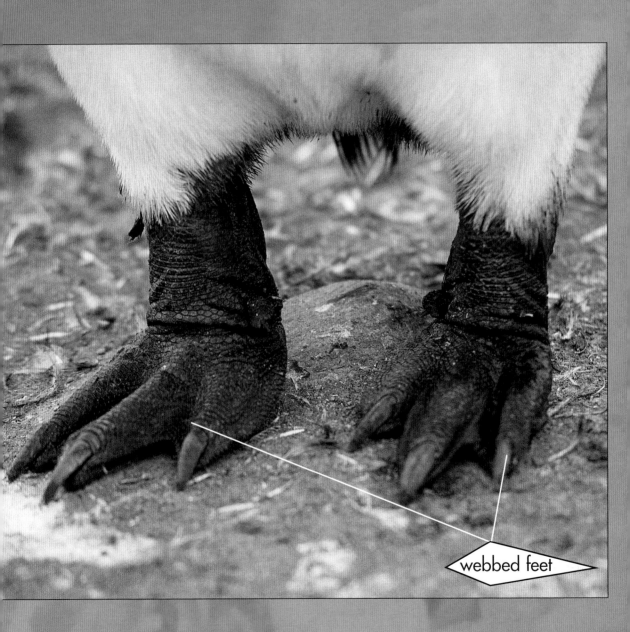

webbed feet

Penguins can slide on the ice on their bellies.
They have long bodies to make swimming easier.

Penguins have short feathers.
The feathers help keep them warm and dry.

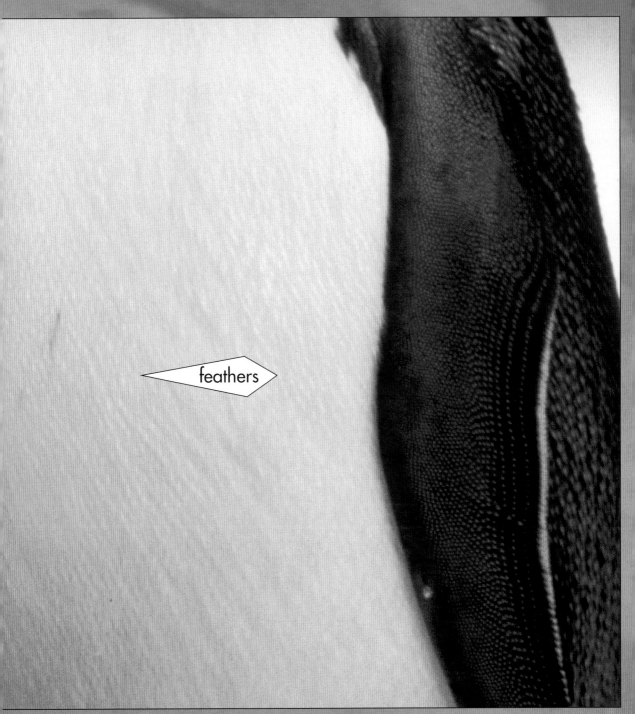

feathers

Baby Penguins

Mother penguins lay eggs.

The eggs must be kept warm so they will hatch.

Some father penguins have a flap of skin called a brood pouch. They keep the egg there so it stays safe and warm.

brood pouch

Baby penguins are called chicks.

The mothers and fathers go into the ocean
to eat fish and other small animals.

While the parents are away,
the chicks huddle to keep warm.

The mothers and fathers find their chicks by making a special sound or call.

Each penguin family has its own call.
That's how they find each other.

The mother and father bring up the food they ate and feed it to the chick.

When a chick is big enough to swim,
it will find food on its own.
Like other penguins, it will spend
most of its life in the water.